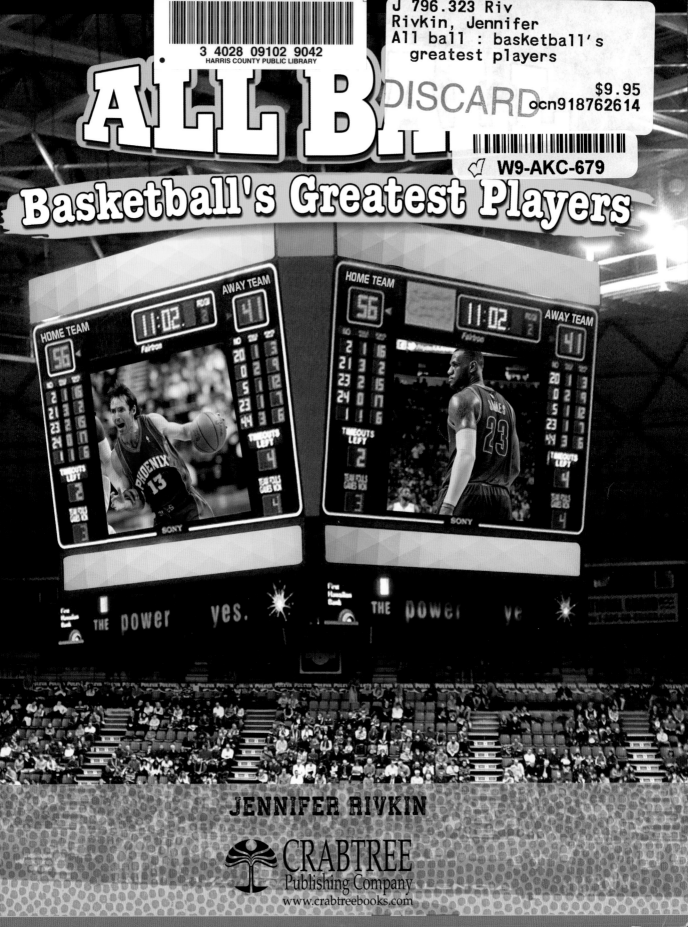

ALL BALL

Basketball's Greatest Players

JENNIFER RIVKIN

CRABTREE
Publishing Company
www.crabtreebooks.com

Author: Jennifer Rivkin

Editors: Marcia Abramson, Kelly Spence

Proofreader: Wendy Scavuzzo

Photo research: Melissa McClellan

Design: T.J. Choleva

Cover Design: Samara Parent

Prepress Technician: Tammy McGarr

Production coordinator: Margaret Amy Salter

Written and produced for
Crabtree Publishing by BlueApple*Works* Inc.

Consultant: Greg Verner, President, Ontario Basketball

Cover images: (background) Michael Jordan, Chicago Bulls,
(center) Steve Nash, Phoenix Suns, (top right) Lisa Leslie,
Los Angeles Sparks, LeBron James, Cleveland Cavaliers

Photographs
Cover: Creative Commons: Keith Allison (middle); Icon
Sportswire: © Ray Grabowski (background), Mark Alberti
(bottom right); Shutterstock: © Photo Works (middle right)

Interior: Corbis: © Bettmann / Corbis (p 7 bottom); ©
Photofest: p 6; Shutterstock.com: © Africa Studio (TOC top,
basketball behind page numbers; © Torsak Thammachote
(TOC); © Dewitt (texture background); © Brocreative (page
top left); © Eugene Sergeev (page top border); © prophoto14
(page bottom border); © Slavoljub Pantelic (Slam Dunk
photo); © Marcos Mesa Sam Wordley (p 4); © efecreata
mediagroup (p 10–11 top); © Aspen Photo (p 18–19 top &
bottom, 30); © Photo Works (p 13, 21, 25); © Natursports (p
22–23 top, 23 bottom); © efecreata mediagroup (28–29 top); ©
Mayskyphoto (28–29 bottom); 123RF: © Eric Broder Van Dyke
(p 22–23 bottom); Keystone Press: © Albert Pena (p 5 bottom,
24, 27 bottom); © Nuccio Dinuzzo (p 9); © Steve Lipofsky (p
10, 14, 18; Zumapress.com / Keystone Press (p 15); © Pedro
Portal (p 16); © Hector Gabino (p 19); © Edward A. Ornelas
(p 20); © Hector Amezcua (p 22); © Stephen Lew (p 23 top); ©
Dennis Van Tine / Geisler-Fotopres (p 26); © Carlos Gonzalez
(p 28); © Anthony Nesmith (p 29 left); © John Fisher (p 29
right); Public Domain: p 7 top, 8, 27 top; Creative Commons:
Chensiyuan (p 5 top); Dave Winer (10–11 bottom); Keith
Allison (p 11, 12, 17)

Library and Archives Canada Cataloguing in Publication

Rivkin, Jennifer, author
     All ball : basketball's greatest players / Jennifer Rivkin.

(Basketball source)
Includes index.
Issued in print and electronic formats.
ISBN 978-0-7787-1534-4 (bound).--
ISBN 978-0-7787-1538-2 (paperback).--
ISBN 978-1-4271-7752-0 (pdf).--ISBN 978-1-4271-7748-3 (html)

     1. Basketball players--Biography--Juvenile literature. I. Title.

GV884.A1R58 2015   j796.323092'2   C2015-903194-X
                                                 C2015-903195-8

Library of Congress Cataloging-in-Publication Data

CIP available at the Library of Congress

Crabtree Publishing Company

www.crabtreebooks.com   1-800-387-7650

Printed in Canada / 082015 / BF20150630

Published in Canada
Crabtree Publishing
616 Welland Ave.
St. Catharines, ON
L2M 5V6

Published in the United States
Crabtree Publishing
PMB 59051
350 Fifth Avenue, 59th Floor
New York, New York 10118

Published in the United Kingdom
Crabtree Publishing
Maritime House
Basin Road North, Hove
BN41 1WR

Published in Australia
Crabtree Publishing
3 Charles Street
Coburg North
VIC 3058

CONTENTS

TAKE IT TO THE NET!

RULING THE COURT

The talented players who become professionals in the NBA (National Basketball Association) or WNBA (Women's National Basketball Association) are the top athletes in their sport. Even at the professional level, there are players who stand out among giants. They are the best of the best. On the court, they are respected (and feared!) by their rivals, admired by their teammates, and worshiped by fans. Off the court, they become household names (who hasn't heard of Michael Jordan and LeBron James?) that become part of basketball history and change the way the game is played.

SLAM DUNK!

Each of the five positions in basketball is assigned a number. Point guards are 1, shooting guards 2, small forwards 3, power forwards 4, and centers 5.

NBA players also represent their country at World Cup.

THE IMPORTANCE OF TEAMWORK

Even superstars can't win games alone. The best teams have strong players working together in each of the five positions. The point guard is responsible for directing plays on the court, making sure their teammates are in position, and setting up opportunities to score. The shooting guard scores points by **driving** to the basket or making long shots. Small forwards must be able to switch back and forth between **offense** and **defense**. The power forward's job is to **rebound** the ball, block shots, and score. Centers play closest to the basket to score and defend.

A basketball game has four quarters. The team with the most points at the end of the game wins.

NEVER GIVE UP!

All pro ballers have to work hard to get to the top of their game. Chicago Bulls' shooting guard/small forward Jimmy Butler had it harder than most. He was raised by a single mother who kicked him out of the house when he was just 13 years old. Butler spent time sleeping on friends' floors and couches. The summer before his senior year of high school, Butler made a friend while playing in a basketball league. The boy's family took him in and gave him the support he never had. He went on to play for Marquette University and was drafted by the Bulls in 2011. Butler was an NBA All Star and won the NBA's Most Improved Player Award in 2015.

BASKETBALL'S FIRST SUPERSTARS

Basketball has come a long way since 1891 when James Naismith invented the game using a soccer ball and peach baskets. The first superstars took basketball to new heights, making it an increasingly popular, fast-paced sport.

DEFENSIVE GIANT

In the 1950s and '60s, Boston Celtics' center Bill Russell dominated the game as a defensive player. Before he went pro, Russell and his team at the University of San Francisco won two NCAA (National Collegiate Athletic Association) titles in 1955 and 1956. The 6-foot-9 inch (2.06 m) superstar continued his streak, bringing home gold as part of the U.S. men's team at the 1956 Olympics. During his 13-year career with the Celtics, Russell became one of the most successful athletes in any sport. He was named the NBA's Most Valuable Player (MVP) five times, was a 12-time All-Star, and led the team to 11 championships. After the 1966 season, Russell took over as Celtics' **player-coach** and became the first African-American coach in the NBA.

*Bill Russell (6) was **inducted** into the James Naismith Hall of Fame in 1975. In 2009, the NBA named the Finals MVP trophy in his honor.*

"Concentration and mental toughness are the margins of victory."
— *Bill Russell*

THE BIG O

Oscar Robertson was one of the first African-American basketball players at the University of Cincinnati in 1957. Throughout university, Oscar was a victim of **racism**. The standout point guard focused on the game and was named college Player of the Year three times, and set 19 records at the school. After being drafted to the NBA by the

Oscar Robertson (14) was inducted into the Basketball Hall of Fame in 1980.

Cincinnati Royals, Robertson started off strong as Rookie of the Year in the 1960–61 season and part of the gold-medal winning team at the 1960 Olympics. In 1961–62, he became the first player in the NBA to earn a **triple-double** average for an entire season. No player has managed to do that since! Robertson was also known for being able to score from anywhere on the court.

GIRL'S GOT GAME

One of basketball's first female superstars was Nancy "Lady Magic" Lieberman. The New York-born point guard dominated her opponents on the court. In 1976, at age 18 she became the youngest basketball player in Olympic history and brought home a silver medal with her team. Over the years, Lieberman played professionally in several leagues including the WNBA. She led the Dallas Diamonds to the WABA (Women's American Basketball Association) Championship in 1984. She was inducted into the Basketball Hall of Fame in 1996.

Lieberman was named Player of the Year twice while playing college ball at Old Dominion University.

HISTORY'S GREATEST TEAMS

When everything comes together for a **franchise**—solid coaching and All-Star players who play well together—it can be magical. The team as a whole becomes a superstar!

BOSTON CELTICS: 1960s

Boston fans are known for their deep-rooted love of baseball, but in the 1960s, the city had a team that managed to turn its attention to the basketball court. In 1957, the Celtics won their first championship. It was the start of one of the greatest streaks in sports history. The team won 11 championships in 13 seasons, dribbling, blocking, and dunking their way to become a sports **dynasty**. Basketball legend Bill Russell was a major part of the winning equation. Some people have called the NBA in the 1960s the "Bill Russell Era." But no one person can win a basketball game on his or her own. The Celtics had a chemistry that helped them to dominate the league. Their streak of eight consecutive championships (between 1959 and 1966) is the longest in history— in any pro sport.

In the 1961–62 season, the Celtics became the first NBA team to win 60 games in a season.

8

CHICAGO BULLS: 1990s

The 1990s brought Chicago a team that won't be forgotten. The Bulls won six titles in eight years between 1991 and 1998. Michael Jordan was a key factor in the team's success. In fact, in 1993 when he retired for more than a year to play baseball, the Bulls lost the championship. Still,

The Bulls won three consecutive titles twice (1991–1993 and 1996–1998).

the Bulls were a superstar team. They had an amazing lineup with several standouts, including Scottie Pippen and Dennis Rodman. Rodman, who couldn't help but be noticed with his tattoos, piercings, and bright hair, made a name for himself on and off the court. Coach Phil Jackson was also legendary. He holds the record (11) for most NBA titles as a coach.

USA BASKETBALL WOMEN'S NATIONAL TEAM

When the U.S.A Basketball Women's National Team steps onto the court, their opponents are afraid…and they should be! Like King Midas, it seems that everything they touch turns to gold. They have won seven Olympic gold medals and nine World Championship golds. The amazing group is made up of some of the best players in the WNBA (Women's National Basketball Association) as well as top college players. The team that was put together in 1995–96 became legendary. They had a record of 60 wins and 0 losses that year.

Point guards are "coaches on the floor," organizing the team and directing plays. The best ballers in this position have incredible **court vision**—with one glance they know where every player is on the hardwood. They have a sense for the game and respond quickly with smart calls, passing, and shooting.

EARVIN "MAGIC" JOHNSON

> "I practiced all day. I dribbled to the store with my right hand and back with my left. Then I slept with my basketball."
> –Earvin "Magic" Johnson

"Magic" Johnson earned his nickname in high school after a sportswriter saw him score a jaw-dropping triple-double game. The magic didn't end there for Johnson, who went on to become the first overall draft pick for the LA Lakers in 1979. That season the team won the NBA championship and Johnson became the first rookie to ever take home the NBA Finals MVP award. He was known for his game sense and amazing passes that confused his opponents and led to three MVP Awards, five NBA Championships, and an Olympic gold medal. Sadly, in 1991, Johnson announced that he was **HIV positive** and retired from basketball. Since then, Johnson has used his celebrity status to raise awareness of the disease.

Johnson was always trying to improve, and he worked on different aspects of his game in the off-season.

STEPHEN CURRY

Basketball is in Stephen Curry's blood. The Golden State Warriors' guard wears the same number (30) that his father, Dell, wore during his own 16 seasons in the NBA. But the younger Curry has stepped out of his father's shadow to make a name for himself as one of the NBA's best shooters. In 2013, Curry set the NBA record for **three-pointers** madein a regular season and then broke his own record in 2015. The two-time NBA All-Star was also the **free-throw** percentage leader in 2011, the same year he won the Joe Dumars NBA Sportsmanship Trophy for fair play and integrity, which is voted on by players in the league.

STATS

Born: 03/14/88
Akron, OH, USA

Position: Point guard
Height: 6 ft 3 in (1.91 m)

Team: #30 Golden State Warriors

SLAM DUNK!

Each year at the end of the regular season, the NBA's top player is named the league MVP. Since the 1980–81 season, the winner is chosen by a panel of sportswriters and broadcasters throughout the United States and Canada.

In 2015, Curry made 77 consecutive three-pointers during practice.

STEVE NASH

Steve Nash rates high on the all-time list of the best NBA players, and many people rank the eight-time all-star as the best Canadian player ever in the league. Nash, who retired in 2015, grew up in Victoria, British Columbia. He played college ball at Santa Clara University, a smaller school in California. Though few fans had heard of him at the time, he was drafted in the first round in 1996 by the Phoenix Suns. They traded him in 1998 to the Dallas Mavericks, where he became a star by his third season. By 2004, when he rejoined the Suns, Phoenix fans were delighted to see him come back, and Nash led the Suns to many playoff appearances. In 2012, he signed with the Los Angeles Lakers. Over his career, Nash led the NBA in assists five times and excelled at shooting free throws and three-pointers. He was twice named league MVP. He also led Team Canada in international play including the 2000 Olympics.

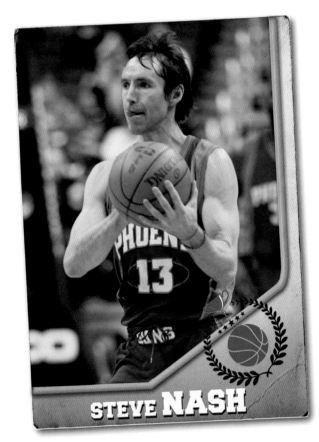

Nash, who has three kids of his own, created the Steve Nash Foundation to help children in poor communities in British Columbia, Canada, and all over the world.

"I think you can get too focused on the championship and forget how rewarding it is to be part of a team."

— *Steve Nash*

SUE BIRD

Championship awards seem to follow Sue Bird wherever she goes. She won two New York state titles in high school, two national championships in college, three gold medals at the Olympics, and two WNBA Championships with the Seattle Storm. Bird is only the seventh athlete ever to win an NCAA title, WNBA championship, and Olympic gold. Bird is a whiz with assists and always puts the team ahead of herself. It's no wonder that she was drafted first overall in the WNBA in 2002 after winning the Naismith Award as College Player of the Year.

SUE **BIRD**

Bird has won the Nancy Lieberman Award as top point guard three times.

STATS

Born: 10/16/80
Syosset, NY, USA

Position: Point guard
Height: 5 ft 9 in (1.75 m)

Team: #10 Seattle Storm (WNBA)

AMAZING POINT GUARDS

- Russell Westbrook has crushed it as point guard. In 2015, he was named MVP of the 2015 NBA All-Star Game where he scored 41 points.

- Chris Paul stars on offense and defense. He was Rookie of the Year in 2006 with New Orleans, won Olympic gold in 2008, and has been helping to turn the Los Angeles Clippers into a top team since 2011.

- Hall of famer Bob "Mr. Basketball" Cousy's talent as a point guard was an important weapon in the Boston Celtics' dynasty of the 1960s. He led the league in assists for eight consecutive seasons, passing with a spectacular style that the NBA had never seen before.

SHARP SHOOTERS

As the name implies, a shooting guard's job is to score points while guarding the perimeter. Players in this position are sharpshooters who can throw the ball with incredible accuracy in any situation.

MICHAEL "MJ" JORDAN

In 1999, Michael Jordan was named the greatest North American athlete of the 20th century by the sports network ESPN. During the Chicago Bulls' dynasty, he led the team to six championships and captured the imaginations of fans who dreamed of being "Like Mike." Jordan dominated because of his competitive spirit and his pure love of basketball. In the midst of his career, however, Jordan retired for more than a year to play minor league baseball. The hardwood drew him back. There was no denying that basketball was his game and Jordan has the awards to prove it, including NBA Rookie of the Year, five regular-season MVP awards, six NBA Finals MVPs, All-Star MVP, ten scoring titles, two Olympic gold medals, and a hall-of-fame induction.

"There is no such thing as a perfect basketball player, and I don't believe there is only one greatest player either...I built my talents on the shoulders of someone else's talent."
– Michael Jordan

Unlike most NBA players, Jordan had a "love of the game" condition in his contract that allowed him to play in the off-season.

JAMES HARDEN

After playing amazing college ball at Arizona State, James Harden was drafted third overall by the Oklahoma City Thunder in 2009. In 2012, Harden won the NBA's Sixth Man of the Year Award, for the league's best performing substitute (sixth man). The same year, he was part of the gold-medal winning Olympic basketball team. He was traded to the Houston Rockets before the 2012-2013 season. While he is famous for his shot-making abilities, Harden is also known for his bushy black beard which has earned him the nickname "The Beard."

SLAM DUNK!

Michael Jordan's black-and-red Air Jordan shoes were banned by the NBA for going against the organization's uniform rules. Every time he wore the shoes, he had to pay a fine of $5,000. Nike paid the bill, and it was worth the company's while, because the media attention made the shoes even more popular.

STATS

Born: 08/26/89
Los Angeles, CA, USA

Position: Shooting guard
Height: 6 ft 5 in (1.96 m)

Team: #13 Houston Rockets

Harden is the first player with at least 200 three-pointers and 700 free throws in the same season.

15

DWYANE WADE

For almost two years, Dwyane Wade had the top-selling jersey in the NBA. Kids wore his name and number, and imagined playing pro ball like "Flash." But his life wasn't always something to dream about. His mother was addicted to drugs and was unable to take care of him. When Wade moved in with his father, he learned discipline… and how to play ball. Wade became a fearless player. He stood out during high school but didn't have the grades to play college ball. Marquette University took him on as a **partial qualifier**; he could attend school and practice with the team but had to sit out games. He worked hard and played the next year. In 2003, the Miami Heat drafted "D-Wade" who has since led the team to three championships.

Born: 01/17/82
Chicago, IL, USA
Position: Shooting guard
Height: 6 ft 4 in (1.93 m)
Team: #3 Miami Heat

AMAZING SHOOTING GUARDS

- Jerry West had a great 14-year career on the court with the LA Lakers. He was an All-Star every year, played in nine finals, and became the only member of a losing team to win the Finals MVP Award (in 1969).

- Clyde "The Glide" Drexler was inducted to the Naismith Hall of Fame in 2004. The ten-time All-Star earned an Olympic gold medal as part of the 1992 "Dream Team," and a championship ring with the Houston Rockets in 1995.

KOBE BRYANT

Kobe Bryant can't remember a life without basketball. His father played in the NBA for eight years and in Italy for eight more. By the time the younger Bryant was in high school, he was a force in the game, too. He broke the southeastern Pennsylvania scoring record and led his team to the championships every year. He was heavily scouted by colleges, but he decided to make himself eligible for the NBA draft right away. The 18-year-old was selected by the Charlotte Hornets and was traded to the Lakers, becoming the youngest player in the NBA at the time. He went on to win three consecutive championships from 2000 to 2002 and two more in 2009 and 2010, along with Olympic golds in 2008 and 2012.

Bryant is a clutch performer, who is able to pull out a win in the last seconds of a game.

STATS

Born: 08/23/78
Philadelphia, PA, USA

Position: Shooting guard
Height: 6 ft 6 in (1.98 m)

Team: #24 Los Angeles Lakers

There's no doubt that Klay Thompson's father, Mychal—a two-time NBA champion—is one proud papa. In 2014, the media nicknamed Klay and Stephen Curry the "Splash Brothers" when they set an NBA record for combined three-pointers (484) for the season.

Small forwards have to be able to do it all—score, rebound, defend, and pass. The best small forwards are skilled at all aspects of the game, but often have special moves they become known for.

LARRY BIRD

Hall of famer Larry Bird grew up in small-town Indiana, and worked on a road crew during time off between colleges, and watched his family fall on hard times. These experiences kept him humble and grounded. Bird practiced day and night to turn his fortunes around—and he turned the Celtics around in the process. When he was drafted in 1979, with a record-setting five-year $3.25 million contract, the team was not doing well. Bird was named Rookie of the Year, and helped the team win three championships in 1981, 1984, and 1986. Bird, with his amazing game sense and the skills to match, was with the Celtics for 13 years before retiring as a player in 1992. In 1997, he became coach of the Indiana Pacers and won NBA Coach of the Year in 1998.

Bird won three consecutive NBA MVP Awards between 1984 and 1986.

LeBron JAMES

"King James" earned his way to basketball royalty as one of the best forwards to ever set foot on the court. The four-time MVP and 11-time All-Star was drafted as the number-one pick by the Cleveland Cavaliers in 2003, straight out of high school. James led the Cavaliers in scoring and, at 20, became the youngest player to win Rookie of the Year. By 28, he was the youngest player to score 20,000 points. At the end of the 2009–10 season, James became a **free agent** and chose to play for the Miami Heat, devastating Cavaliers fans. He was named Finals MVP when he helped the Heat win championships in 2012 and 2013. Now, one of the most famous and influential athletes of all time, James is back with the Cavaliers and the team is hoping to bring home their first championship rings.

LeBron JAMES

SLAM DUNK!

It pays well to be a basketball star. According to *Forbes* magazine, in 2015 LeBron James earned a whopping $64.6 million: $20.6 million from his salary and $44 million from endorsements.

"I think, team first. It allows me to succeed, it allows my team to succeed."
– *LeBron James*

STATS

Born: 12/30/84
Akron, OH, USA

Position: Small forward
Height: 6 ft 8 in (2.03 m)

Team: #23 Cleveland Cavaliers

19

KAWHI LEONARD

Leonard's hands are an astounding 11.3 inches (29 cm) from his thumb to his pinky.

STATS

Born: 06/29/91
Los Angeles, CA, USA
Position: Small forward
Height: 6 ft 7 in (2.01 m)
Team: #2 San Antonio Spurs

KAWHI LEONARD

San Antonio Spurs' forward Kawhi Leonard is uncomfortable with attention. That might not be a problem for him if he wasn't such a superstar on the court—basketball fans can't help but notice him! Leonard is now one of the best scorers and defensive players in the NBA. After playing college ball at San Diego State University, Leonard was drafted by the Indiana Pacers in 2011 and traded to the Spurs the same night. It was a smart trade for San Antonio. The 6-foot-7-inch (2.01 m) baller, who is named after an African prince, helped the team win a championship in 2014 and was the finals MVP.

AMAZING SMALL FORWARDS

- In 2007, after just one season of college ball, Kevin Durant was drafted by the Seattle SuperSonics. He started his career as Rookie of the Year and hasn't slowed down. In the 2013–14 season, his shooting was red-hot and he was named NBA MVP.

- New York Knicks' Carmelo "Melo" Anthony is one of the best offensive players in the league. He holds his team's single-game record with 62 points, and was the 2013 NBA scoring champion. In 2014, Melo signed a $124 million five-year contract with the Knicks.

CANDACE PARKER

Candace Parker can dunk. In high school, she became the first female to win a slam-dunk contest against two future NBA players at the 2004 McDonald's All-American Game. At the University of Tennessee, she was the first woman to dunk in an NCAA tournament game. When the Los Angeles Sparks drafted her in 2008 as the number-one pick, she became the first WNBA player to dunk in multiple games. Parker was the best rookie player in league history, and earned Rookie of the Year and League MVP awards that year. The small forward is a skilled defender and sharpshooter, who has led the league in rebounds and **double-doubles**.

CANDACE **PARKER**

Parker won gold with the U.S. team in the 2008 and 2012 Olympics.

STATS

Born: 04/19/86
St. Louis, MO, USA

Position: Small forward
Height: 6 ft 4 in (1.93 m)

Team: #3 Los Angeles Sparks (WNBA)
UMMC Ekaterinburg (Premier League)

- In the 1970s and '80s, hall of famer Julius "Dr. J" Erving transformed the game of basketball with breakthrough moves such as spins and dunks that fans of the game had never seen before. He was known as the greatest player of his time.

- Scottie Pippen is one of only four players to have their jersey (#33) retired by the Chicago Bulls. His versatility was a major weapon for the team during the six NBA titles they won in the 1990s. Pippen won both an NBA title and Olympic gold in the same year—twice!

The word "power" is in there for a reason. Ballers in this position play aggressively, fighting for rebounds, protecting their basket on the defensive end, and taking close-to-the-basket **post-ups**, dunks, and **layups** on offense.

TIM DUNCAN

Tim Duncan grew up in St. Croix, U.S. Virgin Islands. He started playing in ninth grade, and by the end of high school was a standout. By the time he graduated from Wake Forest University, he had developed an amazing game sense and

TIM **DUNCAN**

was rewarded with the Naismith College Player of the Year and the John R. Wooden Award. In 1997, the San Antonio Spurs selected Duncan first overall. They made a good choice. He's one of the best all-around players in the NBA, and has the awards to prove it: Rookie of the Year, five championship rings, three NBA Finals MVPs, and two NBA MVPs.

Duncan is known for being shy and quiet off the court, and a great clutch player on it.

STATS

Born: 04/25/76
Christiansted,
U.S. Virgin Islands

Position: Power forward
Height: 6 ft 11 in (2.11 m)

Team: #21 San Antonio S

ANTHONY DAVIS

The first thing many people notice about power forward Anthony Davis is his **unibrow**. It's something that Anthony Davis embraces. In fact, he has trademarked the sayings "Fear the Brow" and "Raise the Brow." Once he steps onto the court, fans notice something else about Davis— how he blocks shots and scores points. This year, Davis's **player efficiency rating** (31.1), which is a measure of a player's value, was top in the league. His college coaches expected no less. At the University of Kentucky, where he played one season, Davis led the team to the NCAA championship and was named Most Outstanding Player of the tournament. According to ESPN, the Pelicans plan to offer Davis a five-year contract extension to keep him in New Orleans.

ANTHONY **DAVIS**

Davis was on the gold-medal winning U.S. team at the 2012 Olympics.

STATS

Born: 03/11/93
Chicago, IL, USA

Position: Power forward
Height: 6 ft 10 in (2.08 m)

Team: #23 New Orleans Pelicans

TOWERING CENTERS

Players in this position, also known as "the big man," work their magic close to the basket to score and defend. Centers are generally the tallest and largest ballers on the team.

DWIGHT HOWARD

Howard won the 2008 NBA Slam Dunk Contest, the same year he helped Team USA take home Olympic gold.

Born: 12/08/85 Atlanta, GA, USA

Position: Center

Height: 6 ft 11 in (2.11 m)

Team: #12 Houston Rockets

DWIGHT HOWARD

Dwight Howard became a member of the Orlando Magic in 2004. He had entered the draft straight out of high school where he had been a superstar player, winning many awards such as Gatorade National Player of the Year. He **started** in every game during his rookie year. Howard, who now plays for the Houston Rockets, has led the league in rebounds per game (five seasons in a row), blocks per game, and double-doubles. It's no surprise that the big man with the amazing ability to leap has been an eight-time All-Star and three-time Defensive Player of the Year. Howard also finds time to help children, by funding scholarships and a basketball camp and promoting literacy and fitness.

LISA LESLIE

Lisa Leslie played her way into the Naismith Memorial Basketball Hall of Fame with two WNBA championships, three MVP awards, and four Olympic golds. In 1997, she became one of the first players to join the new WNBA, and she helped build its popularity with fans. Leslie played her whole career for the Los Angeles Sparks. Among her achievements was being the first player to dunk in a WNBA game. Since retiring in 2009, she has been a broadcaster, basketball teacher, and part-owner of the Sparks. In 2011, she was voted in by fans as one of the Top 15 players in WNBA history.

Leslie was selected eight times for the WNBA all-star team.

INCREDIBLE CENTERS

- Wilt "the Stilt" Chamberlain was one of the top scorers in NBA history, leading the league in scoring seven years in a row. In a 1962 game, he earned 100 points in a single game—a record that still stands today.

- Defenders were right to be afraid of Kareem Abdul Jabbar and his trademark "sky-hook." The 7-foot-2-inch (2.18 m) offensive player brought home six championship rings and was six-time NBA MVP and two-time Finals MVP.

- Over the years, Shaquille "Shaq" O'Neal brought more than a few backboards down with his powerful dunks. He received the Finals MVP award each time the LA Lakers won a championship between 2001 and 2003.

STARS OFF THE COURT

Players on the court may be the people hearing their names chanted by the fans, but there are people with positions off the court that are just as important to the game.

PHIL JACKSON, COACH

Phil Jackson is one of the best coaches to ever stand on the sidelines of an NBA game. Between 1989 and 1998, he led the Chicago Bulls to six championships. Next, he worked his magic on the LA Lakers, taking them to five championships between 2000 and 2010. You know you're good when you have more championship rings than fingers! Jackson's coaching style was a unique combination of what he had learned on the court as a player (with the New York Knicks in the 1970s) as well as Eastern philosophy. He encouraged players to **meditate** to increase mental strength, ability to focus, and to better connect to each other. The superstars on his teams, including Michael Jordan, Shaquille O'Neal, and Kobe Bryant, learned a lot from the hall of famer who retired from coaching in 2011.

Jackson won two championships while playing for the New York Knicks, and now serves as their president.

JOHN R. WOODEN, COACH, NCAA

After becoming head basketball coach at UCLA in 1948, John Wooden racked up an unbelievable record of 10 national championships in 12 years. At one point, the team won 88 games in a row! Not surprisingly, Wooden was named NCAA College Basketball's Coach of the Year seven times. Over the years, he inspired his players and taught them how to be successful on and off the court.

"If you're not making mistakes, then you're not doing anything. I'm positive that a doer makes mistakes."
– John Wooden

SLAM DUNK!

Since 1976, the John R. Wooden Award has been given to the college player of the year. The trophy features five figures, each representing one of the five major skills of the "total basketball player"—rebounding, passing, defense, shooting, and dribbling.

Wooden was the first person to be inducted to the Naismith Basketball Hall of Fame as a player (in 1961) and a coach (in 1973).

DICK BAVETTA, REFEREE

Not many people are as dedicated to their job as NBA referee Dick Bavetta, who recently retired at the age of 74. He didn't miss an assigned game during his entire career. He was persistent: If airports were closed due to weather conditions, "the Iron Man of officials" drove for hours through the snow to get to the basketball court. But an NBA career almost didn't happen for Bavetta. When he first tried to get a job reffing games, league executives told him that he was too small and unimposing to do the job. They were wrong—when Bavetta made a call, even the biggest players listened.

*The Brooklyn, New York, native **officiated** 2,635 consecutive regular season games and 270 playoff games in his 39 years with the NBA.*

As of 2014, there were 338 inductees in the Naismith Memorial Basketball Hall of Fame. Are these three future hall of famers? Only time will tell.

ANDREW WIGGINS, MINNESOTA TIMBERWOLVES

Andrew Wiggins of the Minnesota Timberwolves won NBA Rookie of the Year as well as the Rising Stars Challenge MVP at the 2015 NBA All-Star Weekend. Wiggins was selected as the number-one pick in the 2014 draft by the Cleveland Cavaliers, then traded to the Timberwolves before the season began. In his first season, he was named the Western Conference Rookie of the Month four months in a row as he led all rookies in scoring. With his size and speed, he excels at both offense and defense.

STATS

Born: 02/23 /95
Toronto, ON, Canada

Position: Shooting guard
Height 6 ft 8 in (2.03 m)

Team #22 Minnesota Timberwolves

Wiggins, who was born in Canada, played college basketball for the University of Kansas. His father was an NBA player and his mother was an Olympic sprinter.

GIANNIS ANTETOKOUNMPO, MILWAUKEE BUCKS

The Milwaukee Bucks' Giannis Antetokounmpo, a player from Greece, was selected 15th in the 2013 NBA draft by the Bucks. In his first year, he was among the league-leading rookies in scoring, rebounding, steals, and blocks. He improved his scoring in his second year, and fans expect big things from him.

STATS

Born: 12/06/94
Sepolia, Athens, Greece

Position: Small forward
Height 6 ft 11 in (2.11 m)

Team: #34 Milwaukee Bucks

Antetokounmpo competed in the slam-dunk contest and Rising Stars Challenge at the 2015 NBA All-Star Weekend.

CHINENYE OGWUMIKE

Chinenye "Chiney" Ogwumike of the Connecticut Sun was the 2014 WNBA Rookie of the Year. At Stanford University, she set a school and Pac-12 Conference record for rebounds. The Sun made her the first pick in the 2014 WNBA draft. Then she made history with her sister Nneka by becoming the first pair of sisters to be named WNBA Rookies of the Year. Nneka won in 2012. She plays for the Los Angeles Sparks.

Ogwumike was named a WNBA All-Star in her rookie season.

STATS

Born: 03/22/92
Tomball, TX, USA

Position: Forward
Height 6 ft 3 in (1.91 m)

Team: #13 Connecticut Sun

BECOMING A BASKETBALL SUPERSTAR

The athletes in this book have dedicated themselves to the sport and have worked hard to develop the skills to play pro ball. They don't rest once they get there. They train in the off-season, and focus on health and fitness to maintain their edge. It's not enough to be in the league, they have to dominate it!

BASKETBALL FOR FUN

Players who make it to the pros are passionate about the sport. They wouldn't want to be anywhere else but on the hardwood. They have the right idea—whether you are a pro or an amateur, the best reason to play is for the love of the game.

While being tall helps when you want to become a pro, it is not absolutely necessary.

SLAM DUNK!

The five tallest ballers in NBA history all played center.
Manute Bol 7 ft 7 in (2.31 m)
Gheorghe Muresan 7 ft 7 in (2.31 m)
Shawn Bradley 7 ft 6 in (2.29 mm)
Yao Ming 7 ft 6 in (2.29 m)
Chuck Nevitt 7 ft 5 in (2.26 m)

LEARNING MORE

Can't get enough of basketball's amazing superstars?
Check out these books and websites for more information.

BOOKS

Side by Side Basketball Stars: Comparing Pro Basketball's Greatest Players by Christopher Forest, Capstone Press, 2014

LeBron James by Rachel Stuckey, Crabtree Publishing, 2013

Steve Nash by Robert Walker, Crabtree Publishing, 2013

Hoop Genius: How a Desperate Teacher and a Rowdy Gym Class Invented Basketball by John Coy, Carolrhoda Books, 2013

WEBSITES

NBA Hoop Troop

www.nbahooptroop.com

Visit this site to play basketball games, get the most recent scores and stats, and watch videos of players in action.

Basketball Hall of Fame

www.hoophall.com

The best of the best will be remembered forever in the Naismith Memorial Basketball Hall of Fame. Learn more about your favorite hall of famers here.

GLOSSARY

Note: Some boldfaced words are defined where they appear in the book.

court vision Being able to see and understand everything that is happening on the court

defense Acting in a way to keep the other team from scoring

double-double Accumulating a total of 10 or more in two statistical categories (such as points and rebounds) in one basketball game

driving Moving toward the basket

dynasty (sports) A powerful team that is successful for a long period of time

endorsement Publicly saying that you like or use a product or service in exchange for money

franchise A team that is part of a sports league

free agent A professional athlete who is free to sign a contract to play for any team

free throw A shot that is given because of an opponent's foul. It is worth one point and must be made from behind a special line

HIV positive Someone infected with the HIV virus that affects the immune system and may cause AIDS (Acquired Immune Deficiency Syndrome)

inducted To be admitted as a member

layup A shot made from near the basket, usually by playing the ball off the backboard

meditate A mental exercise in which a person concentrates on their breathing or repeating a single word

offense When the team tries to score

officiate To be a referee, umpire, or judge at a game or tournament

partial qualifier A student-athlete who graduated from high school but does not meet all of the academic requirements of the NCCA

player-coach A member of a sports team who both plays and coaches

player efficiency rating A rating system that gives one number for all of a player's contributions

post-up To take up a position against a defender in the post in basketball, while standing with your back to the basket

racism Hatred or discrimination based on race

rebound To catch the ball after a shot has missed going in the basket

started Played in the beginning of the game, rather than being a substitute

three-pointer A basketball shot or field goal from beyond the three-point line

triple-double Double-digits in points, rebounds, and assists

unibrow A single brow resulting from the growing together of two eyebrows

INDEX